WALKING WITH JESUS

Stories From One Hope Church

Edited by Tyrean Martinson

FIRST EDITION

ISBN: 978-0-9889933-7-2

"Let my prayer rise up like incense before you,
the lifting up of my hands as an offering to you."
Holden Evening Prayer, Psalm 141

"O Lord, I cry out to you, "Come quickly."
Open your ears to me when I cry out to you.
Let my prayer be accepted
as sweet-smelling incense in your presence.
Let the lifting up of my hands in prayer be accepted
as an evening sacrifice."
Psalm 141:1-2 God's Word Translation

TABLE OF CONTENTS

INTRODUCTION..1

ONE HOPE..3

HOW I CAME TO FAITH..5

TONGUES LIKE FIRE 7

SINGING IN TONGUES 8

DEVOTED 9

MY ONE HOPE STORY...10

WAIT CALMLY 15

GOD'S DIRECTION 16

SAVED...18

GOD AND THE BROKEN WATER PIPE 19

THE WAY...22

INTO THE LIGHT 23

MADE OF CLAY...24

WHY?..25

THE HOPE...27

A CALL TO SECURITY..28

A CALL TO SECURITY, PART 2 31

GOD'S WAY 33

FAITH AND TRUST … MY GOD 34

SAVED WITH THIS HOPE IN MIND 36

A LETTER OF APOLOGY 37

WE CAN BE SAVED ONLY BY JESUS 41

GOD'S PROTECTION 42

GOD GIVES 44

A LEAP OF FAITH AND GOD'S SUPPLY 45

REDEEMED 47

A PENNY FOR MY HEART 48

A FUTURE 52

TULIP AND EVERLASTING 53

I AM 54

I NEVER LEAVE YOU 55

THE LORD CALLED 56

PRAYERS FOR GUIDANCE 57

BE STRONG AND COURAGEOUS 58

GOD MOMENTS JOURNAL ACCOUNT 59

THIS IS THE WAY 62

A WORD OF GUIDANCE 63

HOPE IN THE LORD 64

PRONE TO WANDER* 65

LET US PRESS ON 69

PRESSING INTO GOD 70

PUT YOUR HOPE IN GOD 72

THE HARDEST THING IN THE WORLD* 73

HOW TO PRAY..80

THE CALL TO FORGIVE 81

THE REASON I CAN STILL FIND HOPE 86

BROKEN, BUT NOT ALONE...87

LIGHT IN THE DARKNESS 91

THE LIGHT OF OUR PRESENT GOD 92

THE BRIGHTNESS AFTER A RAINSTORM....................94

LIGHT REFLECTIONS...95

FAITH IS 96

REAL TO ME 97

AFTERWORD 99

THANKS..100

FINDING YOUR FAITH STORIES 101

INTRODUCTION

By Tyrean Martinson

This project took four months longer than planned. I thought I knew what I was asking for, but realized my call for submissions wasn't clear. I thought it would be easy, then realized I was asking everyone to divulge matters of their inmost hearts. I thought I would just quickly edit, format, and get everything into a publishable file, and I lost papers over Christmas break, found myself swept up in various other projects, and then overwhelmed in the initial wave of fear over the Novel COVID-19. I almost put off the project again.

God showed up in that moment, and I found new vigor, new determination, almost a compulsion to finish this project and finish it as quickly as possible. I still couldn't find those papers. I dug through every file, every drawer, every cabinet, every shelf, and I finally realized I would have to "eat crow" and own up to the loss of those papers. So, I did, and graciously, those whose words had been lost restored them to me via mail and e-mail during a time when we couldn't meet in person.

I think I have all the words sent to me. I hope I do. Each piece, whether poetry or narrative prose, whether true or fiction, is one that is meant for us to read. I think we will all find something here to help us on our own journey, walking with Jesus through different parts of our lives.

As I write this, we're all under stay-at-home orders in Washington State. COVID-19 is making history. We are all making history as we cope with the virus. I hope by the time this book reaches you, the stay-at-home orders will have lifted. If they haven't, I hope this book gives you extra peace and comfort. I also hope it challenges you, if needed.

Within these pages, stories of resilience, hope, and comfort stand next to stories of struggle and trial. God is in all of these moments. God is with us in every emotion. If we are joyful, He is with us. If we are terrified, He is with us. If we laugh, He is with us. If we sorrow and despair, He is with us. God loves us. He loves us all. No matter what. No matter where we are. The Good News is Jesus died for us while we were still sinners. The Gospel is, as Pastor Peter has said, "Jesus + nothing." Our one hope is in Jesus Christ and His righteousness.

ONE HOPE

"There is one body and one Spirit. In the same way you were called to share one hope. There is one Lord, one faith, one baptism, one God and Father of all, who is over everything, through everything, and in everything."

Ephesians 4:4-6 God's Word Translation

How I Came to Faith

By Lauren Colman

I have believed in God as long as I can remember. I can recall praying to God as a preschool lad, asking him to protect me from the creatures lurking in the dark corners, or under the bed in my bedroom after the lights were turned off. My parents were believers. We faithfully went to Sunday School and church every week and gave prayerful thanks before every meal. I was a youth group leader. I knew Christ, or more accurately I knew of Christ, but I couldn't really say I knew Him.

I was very shy as well as physically and socially clumsy, usually chosen tenth for the nine-boy baseball games. Gradually, however, I began to excel academically, then athletically, and by the end of college, I had a degree, a commission as an Army officer, admission to medical school, and an engagement to one of the most popular girls in the neighborhood, someone I couldn't even approach and talk to some years before. But at the same time, I was drifting away from the church, and ultimately, stopped altogether. I don't recall exactly when or why I stopped, but I stopped thinking about God's world and focused on my own.

My fiancé and I were married, I started medical school, and we started a family. We were on our own and things started out well, but by the end of medical school, cracks began to appear in our marriage relationship, and eventually our marriage failed. I lost my wife, family, and hope. I could see our kids every other weekend, but gradually became a smaller and smaller part of their lives. I felt despondent and unloved, or possibly even unlovable.

Eventually, I met another and we started going to church together. Slowly, the messages began making more sense to me and I spent more time reading the Bible. Then, I can recall vividly one Sunday we went to the altar to be served communion by Jack J_____ and I felt mercy and grace and the feeling of hope deep inside me. I think that was the moment I came to know Christ. I have never looked back.

My new partner and I married, raised three sons to be honorable, loving men, and we are still in love with each other and Jesus. That is my story.

TONGUES LIKE FIRE

"Suddenly, a sound like a violently blowing wind came from the sky and filled the whole house where they were staying. Tongues that looked like fire appeared to them. The tongues arranged themselves so that one came to rest on each believer. All the believers were filled with the Holy Spirit and began to speak in other languages as the Spirit gave them the ability to speak."

Acts 2:2-4 God's Word Translation

Singing in Tongues

Anonymous

My college roommate was a charismatic Catholic. She spoke about praying in tongues, singing in tongues, and the rest. One day I asked her about it, so she got out her guitar. I was a new Christian and didn't know anything about tongues.

Before she played anything, we prayed for God to send an interpretation to us both. She sang in tongues. While she was singing, a still small voice said, "God is love."

Since I am a bit of a doubting Thomas, I asked her what she thought it meant. She said, "God is love." I told her that was what I heard also.

DEVOTED

"The disciples were devoted to the teachings of the apostles, to fellowship, to the breaking of bread, and to prayer."

Acts 2:42 God's Word Translation

My One Hope Story

By Cindy Jones

In May of 2017, I loaded my puppy dog into the car and we drove over 2300 miles to Bremerton, WA. I guess it's a good thing we can't see into the future because if I had known everything that I was going to endure across the next two years, I would have tried to avoid it at all cost. Life has always felt hard but I would definitely say the past two years have been the hardest. Upon arriving in Bremerton, things immediately started to fall apart. It's the first time in my life that every single area of my life was affected all at the exact same time. My health, family, safety, job and finances took an immediate downturn.

The house I moved into was plagued with issues and break-ins to other houses on the street were occurring frequently. I was fortunate in that only my mountain bike was stolen. I heard gun shots frequently as a nearby park was a known drug exchange area and those deals didn't always go smoothly. In addition, a man was shot and killed at the end of my driveway. I had just finished walking the dog when it happened. For the next few weeks, I would drive over the large blood stain on the pavement until the rain finally washed it away.

Work had a series of challenges as well. Although I'm not at liberty to discuss those challenges, I can say the parking situation was less than desirable. I park in a dirt lot, down an alleyway that sits between some broken down houses, and on more than one occasion I have had to deal with homeless, or mentally ill, or drug addicts as I walk my mile into work. During the winter, I make this walk in the dark which provides an additional level of anxiety.

My health issues eventually started impacting my work and I took three months of FMLA. During that time, I quickly burned through my savings as I was not receiving a paycheck and my doctor bills were mounting. When I started back to work, it was only part time which continued to place a financial burden on me. Since then, I have had multiple occasions of time off without pay as I have continued to traverse the health issues.

We had four deaths in our family within my first nine months here. I was able to return home for two of the funerals. In addition to the deaths, my mother's health was not good and she was not a candidate for surgery. Trips home have been difficult to achieve due to the financial cost and the required time off from work.

Even my dog couldn't escape the turn of bad luck. She started having seizures which completely freaked me out. She and I have driven through almost every state in the continental U.S. together. Something was wrong with my sweet baby girl and I didn't understand what was going on.

The above is a summary and in no way a comprehensive list of all the challenges I have faced, but I believe it provides an overview of some of the difficulties I have experienced.

I spent the summer of 2017 looking for a church home. I visited many churches in the area and did not find a connection. Through an internet search, I discovered One Hope Church. By the time I visited, I was pretty beaten down. To be honest, I just wanted to sit in the back row, blend in and not be noticed. However, Christine T___ was not about to let that happen. She reached out to me the very first week I visited. By the second week, she and Margaret C___ were praying over me. By the third week, I had an invitation to join their small group. I will be forever grateful for these two beautiful women stepping into my life along with the rest of our small group who had to endure my crying, pain, and overall struggle with everything that was going on in my life. One Hope Church and our TLC (tiny little church) small group has carried me, encouraged me, lifted me up in prayer and loved me in a way that truly expresses Christ in the midst of pain. I will be forever grateful to EVERYONE in our small group as I know and understand how long-suffering they have been with me. I have developed friendships I will treasure the rest of my life.

As I reflect over the past two years, I can see all of the good that came from the bad in a way that only Jesus himself can do. I now possess an inner strength that I have never had before. I have broken through emotional and mental barriers that have held me back my entire life. Medical issues have been brought to light that I probably had prior to arriving here. Even my dog has been cured of her frequent bladder infections and the seizures have stopped. As far as my finances go, God has always found a way. Due to time off without pay, I have only made 50%-65% of my full time pay and somehow the bills still get paid. Due to my connection with One Hope church, I moved to Gig Harbor and no longer worry about safety issues I experienced while living in Bremerton.

Through One Hope, I have made friends that I will cherish for the rest of my life. My faith and trust in God has grown, and for the first time in a very long time, I am part of a church that I truly love. I have overcome obstacles at work that two years ago I would have told you were impossible to overcome. I now possess a greater empathy for others I see struggling. I have learned to be grateful for the "little things" and not take having a roof over my head or food on my plate for granted. I now know more than ever that God truly is the one in charge and it is only by abiding in Him that true value can come from my life.

A few months back while I was attending a One Hope Women's Retreat weekend, I was thinking about everything I had been through since moving to Washington and I felt like God asked me, "Would you have preferred that I had left you as you were?" The answer to that question is a distinct NO! I now experience a joy and happiness that I have missed for most of my life. I firmly believe only God has the capacity to give me such an amazing gift and He used my circumstances and One Hope Church to do it.

WAIT CALMLY

"Wait calmly for God alone, my soul,
because my hope comes from him."
Psalm 62:5 God's Word Translation

God's Direction

Anonymous

After I graduated from college, I was feeling a little disillusioned about the meaning of life. My job was challenging, but also didn't give me the grand meaning of life I had hoped for, and I was less than pleased with the apparent spiritual depth of the church I was attending.

So, I started praying for the church service I attended each week. I would pray that God would speak to me through the sermon and the service, and that I would receive some confirmation about what I should do. Well, each week, the sermon was on very fundamental concepts like "I am the Rock," or the next week, "Lean on Jesus" – very basic things. Each week, I would thank God for that message but ask Him if He could be a bit more specific about what I should do.

After five to six weeks of this, my father was suddenly rushed to the hospital with what turned out to be a deadly aneurism. He was in a coma for a week and then died. My father was my best friend, mentor, rock, and the person I could always rely on. My father was otherwise healthy, and this health issue was unexpected and a true shock.

It turned out that God had heard my prayers all those weeks. And instead of worrying about my career, God knew that my world was about to be shaken … and answered with the sermons I really needed to hear.

SAVED

"The Lord is merciful and righteous.

  our God is compassionate.

The Lord protects defenseless people.

  when I was weak, he saved me.

Be at peace again, my soul,

  because the Lord has been good to you.

You saved me from death.

  you saved my eyes from tears,

  and my feet from stumbling.

I will walk in the Lord's presence

  in this world of the living."

Psalm 116: 5-9 God's Word Translation

God and The Broken Water Pipe

By Lauren Colman

This is a story that, I believe, shows God's mercy and protection. It begins one sunny, cold winter weekend morning right after Christmas when the water pressure in our home fell to nothing. No water for drinking, washing, showering, or even flushing the toilet. Our home was one of twenty-three homes served by a private water system managed by homeowners. It turned out that a pipe near the single well cracked, draining the reservoir and the water mains. Cold muddy water was gushing out of the ground, revealing the location of the broken waterline.

Since it was a holiday weekend, a neighbor and I decided to see if we could patch the line until we could find a plumber to fix the line during the week, so we walked the quarter mile to the site of the break with shovels, clamps, and patch material. We dug down to the pipe, then laid on our stomachs on the cold wet ground, and tried to feel the cracked line in the muddy water so we could attach clamps to hold the rubber patch in place to stop the leak.

19

The problem was that the water line was covered and surrounded with roots of various sizes from the nearby trees and brush. We pulled and tore at the roots and could clear all but one root with our bare hands, but we could not break the one remaining root to be able the secure the clamps. So, we decided to walk to my house to get garden clippers, and perhaps clamps better-sized to fit the pipe than the ones we had.

We returned to the well, only to realize that although we brought back better clamps, we forgot the clippers. We tried again to break the root with our bare hands, but still could not, so we decided to walk to the neighbor's home where he had a well-stocked and organized shop and garden shed with every conceivable tool we might need. We went through his shop, found even better clamps, and returned to the well again only to realize that we had forgotten the garden clippers.

Now by way of background, I was a professional with ten years of postgraduate training in a job that required me to keep and recall lots of complex information on a daily basis. My neighbor was chief machinist at a high-tech research engineering firm whose job also required skill and attention to detail. Still, neither of us could remember to bring back simple garden clipper to cut the root. Anyway, we tried again to free the water line, were finally able to apply the patch and clamps under the root wrapped around the pipe, and stopped the leak. Cold and soaking wet, we walked home to shower and warm up with the restored water pressure.

The following morning, I decided to walk back to the well and the broken water line to inspect our repair. There was still a little water leaking from the pipe but it had cleared, revealing the patch was holding, and that the "root" was actually a 220-volt power line wrapped around the pipe leading to the well.

My heart briefly stopped when I saw that sight, realizing that if I had clipped that line while lying on my stomach on the wet ground, I probably would have been electrocuted. I think that God, always my protector, saw my folly, and erased the thought of bringing clippers to the well twice to protect me.

THE WAY

"Don't be troubled. Believe in God, and believe in me. My Father's house has many rooms. If that were not true, would I have told you that I'm going to prepare a place for you? If I go to prepare a place for you, I will come again. Then I will bring you into my presence so that you will be where I am. You know the way to the place where I am going."

Thomas said to him, "Lord, we don't know where you're going. So how can we know the way?"

Jesus answered him, "I am the way, the truth, and the life. No one goes to the Father except through me. If you have known me, you will also know my Father. From now on you know him through me and have seen him in me."

John 14:1-6 God's Word Translation

Into the Light

By Kathleen Gillespie

Into the light of Jesus,
Come Holy Spirit,
Rest your hand
Upon my shoulder,
Walk me through the labyrinth of my soul,
Poking and prodding,
Awaking
To the
Goodness that surrounds me,
Awakening
Life within me,
Hoping that this moment
Transcends into the light
For the way.

MADE OF CLAY

"Our bodies are made of clay, yet we have the treasure of the Good News in them. This shows that the superior power of this treasure belongs to God and doesn't come from us. In every way we're troubled, but we aren't crushed by our troubles. We're frustrated, but we don't give up. We're persecuted, but we're not abandoned. We're captured, but we're not killed. We always carry around the death of Jesus in our bodies so that the life of Jesus is also shown in our bodies. While we are alive, we are constantly handed over to death for Jesus' sake so that the life of Jesus is also shown in our mortal nature. Death is at work in us, but life is at work in you.

The following is written, 'I believed; therefore, I spoke.' We have that same spirit of faith. We also believe; therefore, we also speak. We know that the one who brought the Lord Jesus back to life will also bring us back to life through Jesus. He will present us to God together with you."

2 Corinthians 4:7-14 God's Word Translation

24

Why?

By Arlie Rue

Graduation was over. A job was awaiting me, beginning in the fall. I had a couple of Vacation Bible Schools to lead over the summer. So, forward I traveled to Eastern Washington to lead VBS for the church in which I was baptized. Life was good. There was a plan.

Oh no, my throat was really sore. Oh well, there was work to be done, so I plodded on. Finally, I went back to Seattle to take up my summer job, BUT that sore throat would not let up.

So, it got my attention.

Diagnosis: rheumatic fever.

Prescription: Bed rest!

Nooooo!

At age twenty-one, to be quiet in bed and up for only bathroom trips? And a job awaiting me? Lord, Lord, why?

WHY?*

At times like this I wonder why
In this bed of affliction, I must lie.

It is easy to look at self and fret,
To forget that God is caring yet.
But I am reminded that my Father above
Has placed me here out of steadfast love.
The furnace of affliction removes much dross
And turns my eyes toward the cross.
There Jesus, my Savior, was crucified
That God, my Father, maybe glorified.
The battle fought, the victory won,
Christ's mission on earth was done.
Therefore, through Him who loves us so,
We have the power to resist each foe.
Why then should I now question God
Since this path before me he has trod?
It is a privilege to be in this school
For he is making me His special tool.
It is for His own Name's sake
That I must this affliction take.

*a.rue 1960

THE HOPE

"God wanted his people throughout the world to know the glorious riches of this mystery—which is Christ living in you, giving you the hope of glory."

Colossians 1:27 God's Word Translation

A Call to Security

By Cindy Jones

I used to be an O__ Database Administrator. I went through a very difficult time in my life partly due to poor choices on my part, and partly due to my company contractually obligating my team to requirements and timelines we could not possibly meet. I was in my early thirties and wanted desperately to be successful as one of the team leads for this contract. There was a six-month period of time where I was unable to obtain two hours of sleep consecutively due to lack of resources and unmanageable timelines. My blood pressure reached a very dangerous range and my doctor told me that if I did not take medical leave from work, I would end up as a stroke victim in a nursing home at a very young age. I took a thirty-day leave of absence.

My life up to that point had always felt difficult to me. I cried out to God and asked him if he really existed, and, if he did, I needed to know it because life had been very challenging and I really didn't care to continue on the path I was on for however much longer I was alive. I was driving home one day shortly after that, and God spoke to my heart and told me he was moving me to security. I positively knew it was God speaking to me and I had never really experienced him before then, but somehow, I just knew that I knew it was him. I was a little confused and asked what he meant by security. Was I going to be a Barney Fife and carry a gun? That didn't seem plausible to me, but all I had to go on was that he was moving me to security. Soon my thirty days were up, and I was back at work.

As I returned to work, people thanked me for going out on medical leave because it caused HR to come in and stop the CEO from driving us so hard for fear of lawsuit. What my Dr. wrote on my medical leave forms had HR very concerned. I met with my manager upon returning to work, and I told him that I didn't know where he stood in his belief of God but that God had shared with me he was moving me to security. My manager informed me that the security department at our company did not have O___ Database Administrators, but only firewall and network people. He also informed me that a move from my team to security would be a cross organizational move and that did not typically happen in the company. In addition, he would have to sign off on the move. I'm pretty sure he thought I had lost my mind and the stress had just been too much for me.

I began speaking to other managers I had worked for on other teams within the company, and one of the managers informed me her husband worked on the security team. She was a Christian and believed what I was telling her. She talked to her husband who put me in touch with his manager. The security team had just purchased a new security tool that had an O____ database as a back end, and they needed an O____ Database Administrator because they did not have any on the team already. After a couple of conversations with the manager of the security team, he reached out to my manager and asked if he would please sign off on me transferring to the team as they really needed my help and expertise. I would have loved to have seen my manager's face when he received that phone call. He did sign off, and I became the very first O____ Database Administrator to work on the security team at my company. I will never forget this as long as I live.

A Call to Security, Part 2

I had a job interview in Seattle today, and as I was waiting for my interview time, I felt like God asked me if I would be willing to share my God story about how I went from being an O_____ Database Administrator to a Security Professional, or if I would just gloss over the details in order to not bring my faith into the interview process?

I said, "You know what God, if presented with the opportunity, I WILL share that story, and if this interview is about me planting a seed and not actually getting a job, then I'm okay with that. I will be okay until you release me from the shipyard."

So, I'm in an interview with the CEO, EVP, and VP of the company. The CEO leans back in his chair and says, "So I'm interested in how you made the jump from being an O____ Database Administrator to being a Security Professional......"

LOL!

My response was, "Well I'm not sure what you are going to think about this, or how you will receive it, but here's my story......" I'll stop there as this would get way too long. So, I had the opportunity to share a God story with the CEO of a Security company in Seattle. When I finished my story, he leaned back in his chair again, looked down at the table and said, "Wow that's quite a story."

I'm pretty sure he hasn't had another interview like mine. The really cool part for me is that I have finally broken through the noise and I'm hearing Him again!

GOD'S WAY

"God's way is perfect!
  The promise of the Lord has proven to be true.
  He is a shield to all those who take refuge in him.
    Who is God but the Lord?
    Who is a rock except our God?
God arms me with strength
  and makes my way perfect.
  He makes my feet like those of a deer
    and gives me sure footing on high places."
Psalm 18:30-33 God's Word Translation

Faith and Trust … My God

By Barbara G. Harris

I am a person who takes charge. I'll do it my way.
Faith and trust are not my long suit, but I am learning and
have been encouraged in God's ways.

Shopping at a grocery store in January, I caught my
foot on an electrical floor outlet, pulled my very full cart
over on my right ankle, and fell back into a beer display.
(My husband loves this part of the story - he looked up and
there I was sitting surrounded by beer.) So embarrassed
and in a hurry to just get out of there, I did not report this -
ever weary of them thinking I wanted to sue. It soon
became evident this was a serious wound.

In the meantime, I visited my dentist, and incurred,
what to me, was a huge expense. As per usual, I finally
said, "God this is Yours, I can't, You can, I ask you to give
me faith and trust that what I do is Your will, Your way and
Your time. I did not worry and fret. I just lived from day to
day with bills piling up.

One day at the grocery store, I decided to report my spill - this was months later. They were very kind in hearing and reporting my story to a company that investigates complaints such as this. A very nice man filled out a form and questioned me in a non-threatening way. I truly expected I would receive a, "Sorry, you had a spill in our store," and maybe just maybe a very little settlement.

Two weeks ago, I received a call from the nice man who was investigating —— the settlement was $4,000. I immediately said my medical bills had certainly not added up to this figure after insurance. He informed me the store wanted to reimburse me for pain and suffering.

My old sinful nature and - can you believe this - I almost refuse to take it. I began to "negotiate" - I'll pay all my bills and tithe. But I know - I know I bring my first fruits.

God is real, God is good, and he cares.

SAVED WITH THIS HOPE IN MIND

"However, not only creation groans. We, who have the Spirit as the first of God's gifts, also groan inwardly. We groan as we eagerly wait for our adoption, the freeing of our bodies from sin. We were saved with this hope in mind. If we hope for something we already see, it's not really hope. Who hopes for what can be seen? But if we hope for what we don't see, we eagerly wait for it with perseverance."

Romans 8:23-25 God's Word Translation

A Letter of Apology

By Cindy Jones

I have been trying really hard to stay dedicated to exercising, but the other night it was 10:30 before I completed my "to do" list for the day and could think about exercising. I did not want to walk in the dark across the property to the apartment gym, so I drove. The only problem was that I could not find a close spot that was lit. I knew I was taking a calculated risk as I pulled into one of the covered spots, hoping it was either unassigned, or that the owner would not be home in the short time I was parked there. It was a bad miscalculation.

When I walked back to my car, a very angry man had me blocked in, and was in the process of calling a tow truck. HE WAS IRATE. He was wearing an EMS uniform, said he had just gotten off a shift, and didn't this "blank blank blank blank ...." He, finally, pulled up, and let me back out. I was scared and didn't know if he would follow me to see which apartment I lived in, so I left and drove around for a little bit. It was after 11pm, so I didn't call anyone. He had written my plate number down, and as angry as he was, I didn't know if I would still have a completely intact car in the parking lot the next morning.

When I got home, I felt horrible because I did know better, and there is no telling what this guy was exposed to on his shift. His spot being taken was probably the icing on the cake that made him pop. So, I was trying to think how to turn this into a positive for the guy, if at all possible. I wrote him an apology note which I took by the office, and asked them to pin it to his door. I also told them I would like to pay for his parking for the month. While I was writing the apology note, I prayed and asked God to use this to help restore this man's faith in humanity. For me to know this guy was struggling with faith in people was not wisdom on my part; I am sure it was knowledge the Holy Spirit gave me.

The office personnel told me this guy had real anger issues, and they had had issues with him in the past. They also stated that they had several recorded conversations of this guy tearing into people, and they could only imagine what all he said to me. They really did not want me to pay for his parking, but I insisted. I, myself, felt it was a little overkill, and the apology note should be enough, but I also knew God was telling me to do this and that it was non-negotiable, so I figured He had a plan to use it.

Later, I received an apology note from the man. He spoke about how my kindness had touched him, how I had "helped to restore his faith in humanity," and that he wished he had responded with a more Christian response. Remember what I said I prayed for?

I went by the apartment office to let them know I had gotten the note, and they said they had been talking about it all afternoon. Everyone in the office was in awe of how he "humbly" came in, showed remorse for the way he had treated me, and asked them to pass this note along to me. They even told me that they told him they would not pass the letter along until they knew it did not say anything mean in it. He assured them it was an apology, and repeated again how bad he felt. The office told me that I had no idea how big of a deal this was because they would have never thought in a million years this guy would write an apology note, or be remorseful about anything. He also refused my payment for his parking.

So, I made a mistake, and I am sure I will continue to make mistakes. The great thing is that God took my mistake, and still used it for His good. I wake up every day in awe with the life God has given me, and how He allows me to participate in what He is doing.

That apology letter is going in my God Moments notebook.

You know that situation could have turned out so differently. He was so angry that I was prepared to pepper spray him if he got out of his vehicle and stepped toward me. He had me blocked in, so getting in my car and driving away was not an option. I'm so thankful it turned out the way it did.

WE CAN BE SAVED ONLY BY JESUS

"Then Peter, because he was filled with the Holy Spirit, said to them, 'Rulers and leaders of the people, today you are cross-examining us about the good we did for a crippled man. You want to know how he was made well. You and all the people of Israel must understand that this man stands in your presence with a healthy body because of the power of Jesus Christ from Nazareth. You crucified Jesus Christ, but God has brought him back to life. He is the stone that the builders rejected, the stone that has become the cornerstone. No one else can save us. Indeed, we can be saved only by the power of the one named Jesus and not by any other person.'

After they found out that Peter and John had no education or special training, they were surprised to see how boldly they spoke. They realized that these men had been with Jesus. When they saw the man who was healed standing with Peter and John, they couldn't say anything against the two apostles."

Acts 4:8-14 God's Word Translation

God's Protection

By John Schuler

I had worked as a residential carpenter for several years; I was about twenty-six years old. There had been an accident the day before at work, where a forklift had crushed a man's foot. The talk was about whether the steel toe in his boot helped him, or not, because it bent into his toes. I was on the second floor of a building we were building, and I decided to pray for protection and that there would be no accidents that day for the whole crew. I went to the first floor and walked out the door leading to the ground outside, when two carpenters were moving a movable scaffold.

A plank was at one end on a ladder jack that is stationary, and the other end was on the movable scaffolding. The carpenters were not thinking, and as I was walking under the movable scaffolding, they were moving it. The scaffolding was three pieces high, that is fifteen feet. The plank was rented by the company for standing on. It took two men to comfortably carry it.

It hit me flat on my head. Nothing happened. It should as likely have killed me than nothing happening. It bounced off my head and to the left of me, not even hitting my shoulder. Not a headache, completely not one pain resulted from the hit.

Shortly after this, I was visiting a college when some students were tossing a soft ball. I was sitting on the ground, the ball bounced, hit me in the forehead, and it hurt. I thought of the plank, and I laughed.

GOD GIVES

"God gives seed to the farmer and food to those who need to eat. God will also give you seed and multiply it. In your lives he will increase the things you do that have his approval. God will make you rich enough so that you can always be generous. Your generosity will produce thanksgiving to God because of us. What you do to serve others not only provides for the needs of God's people, but also produces more and more prayers of thanksgiving to God. You will honor God through this genuine act of service because of your commitment to spread the Good News of Christ and because of your generosity in sharing with them and everyone else. With deep affection they will pray for you because of the extreme kindness that God has shown you. I thank God for his gift that words cannot describe." *2 Corinthians 9:10-15 God's Word Translation*

A Leap of Faith and God's Supply

By Pat Lelvis

I was twenty-three years old. I had applied to World Mission Prayer League for missionary service in Pakistan and been accepted. I had a one-way ticket via freighter to Pakistan, and I had $150 in Travelers' Cheques in my pocket. My first term would be five years.

World Mission Prayer League is a "faith" mission, which means no one is hired by the Mission, and no one is promised any financial support. We all just pray and look to the Lord to supply our needs month by month.

A very small group of family and friends saw me off at the train station in the UP of Michigan for the first leg of my journey. In New York, I met up with the rest of our missionary team, two couples with five small children between them.

When I got to my cabin on the freighter, I found an envelope with my name on it. Inside was a letter from the Sunday School teachers of Morgan Avenue Lutheran Church in Minneapolis. First, there was a simple greeting, wishing me well. Then, the letter explained, that the small Sunday School (about one hundred students) was pledging to supply my Living Allowance ($65.00 per month).

The letter went on to say that just as I was taking a "step of faith," so were they. They explained that their Sunday School was always in debt. (In those days, Sunday schools took up an offering each Sunday with which they purchased their books and other supplies.) At a recent Sunday School Teachers' meeting, there had been considerable discussion about the ongoing debt. Suddenly, one of the teachers had said, "I know what we should do, we should support a missionary." I know, it sounds crazy, even as I write it now. And, at that very meeting, they decided to do just that, and they decided they should support me.

Every month for fifteen years, they faithfully supported me. When I came home on my first leave (after five years in the field), I met with those Sunday School teachers. They recounted how there had been enough in each month's offerings to pay the pledged amount, and furthermore, they were never in debt again!

REDEEMED

"In him (Jesus) we have redemption through his blood, the forgiveness of our trespasses, according to the riches of his grace, which he lavished upon us, in all wisdom and insight making known to us the mystery of his will, according to his purpose, which he set forth in Christ as a plan for the fullness of time, to unite all things in him, things in heaven and things on earth."

Ephesians 1:7-10 ESV

A Penny for my Heart

By Susan Buethe

Did you know the United States of America has the
only currency with the words, "In God we Trust" on it?
From the smallest amount, a penny to the largest thousand-
dollar bill, it reads "In God We Trust."

I have heard of people seeing a penny on the ground,
and not even bending down to pick it up. I have seen them
swept up in a dustpan to be thrown into the trash bin at the
next passing. Only one penny does not add up to much: one
cent. A hundred pennies become a whole one dollar. The
small things do matter, and if you have enough pennies,
then they can be combined to make a greater amount. To
me, the penny has brought assurance in knowing God is
near.

Pennies have had significance in my life for several
years. I even have an image of a penny on the wallpaper on
my cell phone. Anyone close to me will assure you that
they have appeared and spoken to me in various
circumstances from heartbreaking sadness to the highest

joy-filled moments and those in between. I have found them in a variety of locations. Most often, I will find them in the oddest of places and have known that God is reminding me to trust in him, just as the penny says. I have been known to burst out loud laughing at finding one, holding it up to whomever is near to share, "I just found a penny!" In other times of sadness, I have only whispered a prayer of "Thank you, Jesus," and slipped it into my pocket to hold close and touch throughout the day as a reminder that God loves me and has heard my plea for guidance, or relief of a burden I have yet to surrender, or the pure joy, or peace that only He can provide.

My father passed away from acute COPD. We had him cremated. His remains were to be placed in a columbarium at the local Veteran's Cemetery. At the time of his ceremony, the space had not completed construction and he was to remain on a shelf for at least six weeks. I remember hearing that information and being sad that his remains would not be secured until then.

Several weeks passed before family members and I had the opportunity to visit his permanent resting place. His favorite flower was yellow roses. I found the spot and placed the yellow roses close to his plaque in remembrance of him.

After spending a few minutes at the location, I wandered down to the flag pavilion that had also been recently completed. There were flags and bronze markers for each of the branches of military service. As I stopped to examine each one, I found myself standing in front of the bronze marker for the Navy. My father had served in the Korean Conflict and had been honorably discharged from the Navy. There on the top of the marker was a penny. I started to weep at the sight of that penny! God knew I needed to know my Daddy was right where he needed to be in the arms of Jesus. I felt overwhelming peace in this small act of assurance from God. How did it come about that there on that particular day, at that particular moment, and that particular marker was there a penny, just resting on the edge and waiting for me to find it? The family members with me just shook their heads in wonderment. Of course, you found a penny!

Fast forward five years later, family had arrived from out of state, and on their list of things to do was to visit our father's resting place. We found flower vases and water, and placed a bouquet of yellow roses close to his plaque. On closer inspection, I found a penny. A bit of a distance away, someone else found another penny, and then another penny was found a few feet away. We started to laugh! In the end, we had found several pennies. We stacked the pennies on top of his plaque. The interesting part of this story is that we had come directly from a coin collector where we had just sold our father's coin collection. The coin collection spanned decades and consisted of a variety of coins and paper currency, both domestic and foreign. The opportunity had arisen since we were all in one place and enough time had passed, we felt comfortable with parting without our father's extensive coin collection. Once again, God had given us the assurance that it was the right thing to do and it was okay to part with the valuable collection.

We trusted in God just as the penny reminds us to do.

A FUTURE

"'I know the plans that I have for you,' declares the Lord. 'They are plans for peace and not disaster, plans to give you a future filled with hope.'"

Jeremiah 29:11 God's Word Translation

Tulip and Everlasting

By Tyrean Martinson

A tulip stands tall

Amongst the flowers

My mother calls everlasting.

Pink, rounded edges on a straight stem,

Surrounded by purple tufts branching upwards and

      outwards.

Life shown, fleeting and forever,

Precious in any form, for any season,

Reminding me to measure this world

Against the length of eternity.

When the tulip dies, the everlasting will live.

*reprint from Light Reflections: A Poetry Collection

I AM

"God answered, 'I will be with you. And this will be the proof that I sent you: When you bring the people out of Egypt, all of you will worship God on this mountain.'

Then Moses replied to God, 'Suppose I go to the people of Israel and say to them, 'The God of your ancestors has sent me to you,' and they ask me, 'What is his name?' What should I tell them?'

God answered Moses, 'I Am Who I Am. This is what you must say to the people of Israel: 'I Am has sent me to you.'"

Exodus 3:12-14 God's Word Translation

I Never Leave You

By Kathleen Gillespie

Involved,
I AM
In
Your life.
Your journey
Mapped,
Each inch
Haphazard
Fit
In a fallen
Nation
With unraveling edges.
Trust
My way
In the midst
Of
Messy imperfection.
Stay aware
Of me.
Remember,
I never
Leave you.
I AM.

THE LORD CALLED

"The Lord called Samuel a third time. Samuel got up, went to Eli, and said, 'Here I am. You called me.'

Then Eli realized that the Lord was calling the boy. 'Go, lie down,' Eli told Samuel. 'When he calls you, say, 'Speak, Lord. I'm listening.''So, Samuel went and lay down in his room.

The Lord came and stood there. He called as he had called the other times: 'Samuel! Samuel!' And Samuel replied, 'Speak. I'm listening.'"

1 Samuel 3: 8-10 God's Word Translation

Prayers for Guidance

Anonymous

After college, I was about to drive to my new
hometown to find an apartment but I stopped halfway to
pick up my college roommate. She was going along to help
me look. As we visited, I told her how I wondered if this
new career was the move God wanted me to make.

She instantly replied, "Let's ask Him!" So, we prayed.
She asked God to confirm in so many words what I should
do. That night, I dreamed about three projects I would work
on at my new job, and then I woke up.

While we drove the next day, I told her about the
dream in great detail. When we arrived at my new
workplace to meet my new boss, he announced he would
be on vacation for the next two weeks so he wanted to tell
me about my assignments, so I could get started without
him. He said my friend could stay. Then, he described the
projects. My new boss described in great detail the three
projects exactly as they appeared in my dream.

As he spoke, I looked at my friend as her jaw dropped. When she saw me look over, all she said was, "Is that good enough for you?" Then, we went apartment hunting and I found a lovely new apartment home.

BE STRONG AND COURAGEOUS

"Only be strong and very courageous, faithfully doing everything in the teachings that my servant Moses commanded you. Don't turn away from them. Then you will succeed wherever you go. Never stop reciting these teachings. You must think about them night and day so that you will faithfully do everything written in them. Only then will you prosper and succeed.'

'I have commanded you, 'Be strong and courageous! Don't tremble or be terrified, because the Lord your God is with you wherever you go.'"

Joshua 1:7-9 God's Word Translation

God Moments Journal Account

By Cindy Jones

November 2006 – September 2007

God laid it on my heart to create a Christian resource library for Bethlehem House. As of September 23, 2007, over three hundred new and used books have been collected and donated to Bethlehem House. I wrote letters to several organizations and many donated such as Charles Stanley, Bob Coy, Crown Financial, Focus on the Family, etc. There were many individual contributors from the community as well.

December 2006

Bethlehem House needed two men sponsored for Christmas. I told Judi I would do it without really knowing how it would get accomplished. Malvin and his small group agreed to buy clothes for one of the guys and my community group bought clothes for the other guy. The envelope from my small group had a $100 bill in it along with several $20s!

January 28, 2007

Last Friday night, Edye and I purchased a shelf of books from Family Christian bookstore for $21.50. They were going out of business and just wanted to get rid of as much as possible. Most of the books are going to Bethlehem House for their resource library that I am putting together, but there were twenty-seven Fields of the Fatherless books which didn't seem applicable for Bethlehem House. Edye said she had a friend who worked with orphans so she called and left her a message that we had the book for her if she wanted it. She called back with much excitement because she and her husband had just been to a seminar on working with orphans and that was the number one recommended book to get for reading material. Things are really tight for them right now so she chose not to purchase the book and asked God to provide it for her. He not only provided her with the book, but she is getting all twenty-seven of them!

Spring 2007

I felt compelled to buy a particular Billy Graham book back in January, but wasn't sure who was supposed to get it. It stayed on my shelf for three months. I had dinner with a friend one night and she mentioned that she needed some books for her dad who had recently been put in jail for DUIs. She said her dad always felt like God was calling him to preach but he just couldn't commit to that lifestyle, so it seems like he has been running from God most of his life. Anyway, the book immediately jumped into my head and I knew I was supposed to give her that book along with a book on alcoholism which I had just purchased the day before. When she saw the books, she got real excited and said that Billy Graham was her dad's favorite. The book was called *Peace With God.*

September 14, 2007

The Lord led me to purchase sixteen Celebrate Recovery Bibles for Bethlehem House, however, the total was $326.00, and that was going to be a significant amount concerning how much money I had already spent that month. God led me to send an email out to friends at work and church. All but $50 of the money was raised for the Bibles and I covered the $50 without any problem. Judi L____ was extremely excited about the donation.

THIS IS THE WAY

"You will hear a voice behind you saying, 'This is the way. Follow it, whether it turns to the right or to the left.'"
Isaiah 30:21 God's Word Translation

A Word of Guidance

Anonymous

One afternoon as my fiancée was taking a nap, I sat looking at him. I had an open attitude but was not saying a prayer in the usual sense. In the clearest, simplest way, I was just thinking to myself, "Who is this person? Is this the person I should marry?" Almost immediately, a still small voice said, "This is a good man." We have married for twenty-six years now.

HOPE IN THE LORD

"Even young people grow tired and become weary,
    and young men will stumble and fall.
Yet, the strength of those who wait with hope in the
Lord
        will be renewed.
        They will soar on wings like eagles.
            They will run and won't become weary.
            They will walk and won't grow tired."
Isaiah 40:30-31 God's Word Translation

Prone to Wander*

By Grace Rolle

March 13, 2018*

It has been a long time since I have written. Maybe I was procrastinating, maybe I was intimidated, maybe I was just straight up scared of what He was calling me to write. The truth is, I have been sitting on this lesson the Lord taught me for two months. I knew as soon as it was revealed to me that I should share it, but fear is a liar and convinced me it wouldn't be good, that no one would care. But, I'm learning a little something about obedience as well. So here I am, all over the place but unrelenting and unwavering- just as promised.

I was saved five* years ago. It has been the craziest adventure, but also the most beautiful. Through all my years of following Jesus, I have poured my heart out hundreds of times, cried out to him, and asked him countless questions. The one question I had always gone back to was "Where are you, God?". I would cry out to him with all my heart, and I would mean it. My heart would ache for Him, I was desperate for Him to be with me in that moment. I followed this pattern for years. I would run back to this dance with God and then I would be back on track and then just like that months later I would be back on my knees crying out to Him.

I remember a few months ago I was driving in my car after a long week, feeling tired and empty, when at a stop light I couldn't fight it anymore and I began to cry. Desperate, I cried out "Where are you, God? I Can't feel you. Reveal yourself to me." The light turned green and I was still a mess, but I remember so clearly, "Where are you, Grace?". What did that mean? My mind started racing, what could that even mean? It makes no sense! Here I was, crying out to God and he asked me the same question? That wasn't an answer! But, it ended up being one of the biggest lessons I would learn in my life so far.

I remember getting home, sitting on my bed and thinking. I was feeling empty. It felt like a miracle that I had even made it this far in this week while keeping it (somewhat) together. Where was I? I was right here. Couldn't God see me waving my hands in the air? I was right where he left me. Where was I? The question seemed more ridiculous the more I thought of it. Then it hit me. God doesn't move. He doesn't change. He doesn't leave.

He is with us where we go, and these scriptures support it. (Joshua 1:9, Hebrews 13:8, Matthew 28:20, Psalm 23:4). I had been living so far into this victim mentality that I had become so convinced that God was leaving me, when all along I was the one wandering. I was the one walking away. In the busyness and stress of my life, I had begun to walk away from God and continued to place the blame on Him. I had become the Victim. I had learned about myself that this was a tendency of mine, but I never knew how deep it ran until I was face to face with this scenario. Woe was me. I was stressed out, and I couldn't hear what God was saying to me. I was crying out to Him, but I turned my back when it was time to hear his answer. I was forcing my relationship with him to be one sided.

When I realized this, my soul ached. Conviction flooded my mind; how could I have done this? How did I get to this point? I released it all to him that night, I cried out my repentance and I quieted my soul and for the first time in weeks, I enjoyed his presence. I read my bible. I prayed diligently. I worshiped. And God thawed my heart that had become hardened. Our God is a kind and merciful God, who grants us Grace daily when we don't deserve it and I am so thankful. (Now would be a good time to listen to Reckless Love by Bethel)

It is so easy to turn away from the Lord without even realizing it. One of my favorite hymns "Come Thou Fount" says it better than I ever could;

"Prone to wander, Lord I feel it. Prone to leave the God I love. Here's my heart Lord, Take and seal it. Seal it for thine courts above."

Wandering does not mean that you Love God less, I loved God with every part of me then, just as I do now. It is in our human sinful nature to wander, when we know it is best to keep close and hold fast to the Lord.

My prayer for you is that you seek the Lord. Before you ask Him where He is, ask yourself where you are. Where is your heart at? Where are your priorities? Where has your joy been laying? Have you made time for the Lord this week? Have you quieted your soul? Be unwavering and unrelenting in the pursuit of our sweet Jesus my friends. This life and this road is messy, but Jesus has a way of making beautiful things out of dust.

Reprint from Grace All Over the Place

LET US PRESS ON

"Let us know; let us press on to know the Lord;
    his going out is sure as the dawn;
he will come to us as the showers,
    as the spring rains that water the earth."
Hosea 6:3 ESV Translation

Pressing Into God

By Cindy Jones

I wanted to share something amazing that happened at
work today. One of the guys I work with started sharing
some things he has been struggling with lately. Given the
environment we work in, I was really shocked that he was
being so vulnerable. This six-foot something, ex-military
guy broke down and just started sobbing. He said he knew I
was a Christian and that for the past four years he has been
pushing God away. He asked me to please pray for him,
and as his sister, would I please help him to find Christ
again?

I immediately felt like everything I had been through
in the past year just culminated to this exact point. I keep
index cards with scripture verses at my desk and would
read through them several times a day. Well, I handed those
over to him, as well as emailing him a few Bible verses
from my desk. I told him about the importance of pressing
into God and how we need to learn to abide in Him. I
talked to him about the importance of being in God's Word

daily along with prayer so we have the armor we need to withstand the enemy.

We probably talked for an hour. He called me at my desk right before I was leaving and said, "Cindy, thank you so much. Thank you for being my sister. Thank you for being a Christian. Thank you for being you. You have no idea....."

As I was hiking the mile to my car in the pouring down rain, I felt like God said, "I'm asking you to be a light in a very dark place, and in the process, I'm changing you as well. I will give you everything you need." The moment I got to my car and slid into the driver's seat, the rain stopped and the sun came out. I looked up to heaven, giggled and said, "You're a funny man, God!"

THAT...RIGHT THERE...is worth every single thing I have been through this past year.

PUT YOUR HOPE IN GOD

"Why are you discouraged, my soul?
 Why are you so restless?
 Put your hope in God,
  because I will still praise him.
  He is my savior and my God."
Psalm 42:11 God's Word Translation

The HARDEST Thing in the World*

By James Estin

You see your child through the prison bars of a hospital bed and it is the hardest thing in the world. They are not really prison bars, of course - you know that - they're for her protection, that's all. Those tiny hands grip the bars and she staggers to a stand, twenty-nine inches towering in stature. She cries and you reach through and in some useless attempt at comfort, taking precaution not to tear the IV from her delicate arm.

She calms and you release for a moment, because twisting your wrists through the bars is painful, and because your knees buckle under you. Last night was Hell on earth, saturated with hacking and coughing and barking, a medieval sort of torture, clanging you awake each time you nodded off. You collapse in an orange vinyl chair by the window, where filtered sunlight strains through dirty panes, and the vinyl squeals beneath your weight. You lift the single-button channel changer, an obnoxious device that only moves the TV upward a single channel at a time, this heavy, clunking box dangling a power cord that could recharge an small electric car. You wonder why hospitals, with all the money they make, can't afford something as simple as a decent remote.

You flip past anything you might remotely wish to watch, and so you have to flip through the channels all over again, until you settle on Brit Hume calmly delivering the events of the day, the news of yesterday slightly retold. You like Brit Hume. You tell yourself he is one of the few serious journalists left on the planet. But your child cries; she doesn't want to watch Brit Hume, and you sigh your exhausted, sleep-deprived, worry-stricken-parent sigh, and click up and around the Ferris wheel of channels until you find Disney, or Nickelodeon, you aren't really sure because they're all the same to you now. Some poor soul in an enormous brown bear suit wags his furry head at the camera and bends to talk to a pair of purple otter sock puppets, and she laughs and you drop the changer. It falls to swing back and forth like a pendulum beneath the complicated-looking mechanism that lifts and lowers her prison-bed. You didn't really want to watch TV anyway, you just have to wait, and the waiting is the hardest thing in the world.

So there you sit - with your spouse, perhaps, or maybe alone - and you say nothing, because what is there to say? Your child's heartbeat sounds from the monitor on the wall like a quick metronome. You shuffle about in your squeaky chair and stare out the open door, where orderlies push linen carts and nurses walk by in their just-right gait, dressed in pale blue cotton that take away personality, sexuality, humanity. Occasionally another parent walks by, and you drop your gaze to avoid their eyes. They usually walk alone, but sometimes they push past a wheelchair with a small, hunkered body in it, bent over and poked with tubes. You know them for who they are - they do not wear pale blue clothes, they dress like you, in jeans and sweatshirts or whatever they happened to throw on when they came.

You don't want to know these parents of the damned, who pace their vigils while their children suffer unimaginably in the rooms around you. To know those souls is to become a citizen of this place, and you don't want to become a citizen of this place. You are thankful it is here, yes, of course – glad it is there but you sure as hell don't ever want to need it. One shuffles by, a boy clinging to her arm, staggering under the load of his disease – cancer. you surmise, by the shaved head. You catch her eye and it's the moment you dread, because in that moment you see everything you don't want to know.

I was you, once, those eyes say. I sat in one of these rooms for the first time too, waiting to hear the test results, to know what my future would hold. I never thought it would be this, no never, I never believed I would wake up on a beautiful spring day all those years ago and go in to wake up my boy and find his bed full of bloody vomit, would find him doubled over from some unknown demon tearing at his abdomen, would hear him coughing so hard he cried in between attacks. You knew, didn't you? You knew that it was more than nothing, that it was something alien and sinister, and here you are. While the sun shines on the rest of the world, we stand in blackness, don't we? I know you. I was you, once. You could be me.

When the doctor returns, you hope he is alone. More than one means your child's case is interesting. You don't want her case to be interesting. You realize you are at the fulcrum of your life, that in those next minutes you will know your fate, her fate, you will learn whether you will join those people who shuffle the halls day and night, pushing your child around from one medical experiment to another, from one horrific machine to another, as a participant in some sterile religious order. Wandering from test to test because deep down maybe even the doctors don't know either, though they never tell you that, never even imply it, but you can read it in their faces. Even the doctors don't know sometimes, and then you understand what it really comes down to, what is in fact the hardest thing in the world: that in all our glory of knowledge and technology, we do not always know what to do. That we are in those moments held in the hand of God Himself and we do no control our fate, we do not choose happiness or sorrow, we are utterly at the mercy of Someone above and beyond all understanding...and that sometimes, for some unknown reason that we cannot fathom, that Someone chooses us to suffer. And all the while the world goes on as it did while everything you know falls apart, your home, your job, your family, your place in the social order, all slipping quietly away and you never even see it go. It's the moment of divergence, and you have no control at all. You dread that moment's arrival, because until it comes a chance remains that all will turn out well - but in that moment all possibility collapse to one reality. You don't want that moment to come, but come it will.

The doctor returns. He is alone...he is accompanied by others...and dressed in a casual knit shirt that says, hey, just dropping in before I head out to the greens to let you know everything is fine...they are dressed in long white frocks, garments of their Priesthood...he remains standing...they sit down...and he smiles...they do not smile...He tells you the tests came back normal...showed something unusual...and that it looks like it's just a nasty bug...it's not something they've seen before...More testing is unnecessary...necessary...and after a bit of observation, she can go home...they go over some things, you better go home, get some rest, then come back with your suitcase and prepare to stay awhile...

She is freed from her prison and defrocked of her little gown...watches you from behind the bars, knuckles white where she grips them...You pick her up and dress her...reach through, touch her hair...and then you are out of there...in there...almost as fast as you can be, before she really catches something, before they have a chance to change their minds and drag you back...and you return with that suitcase, you move into Hell, you await a parole that may never come...You sit beside her, and tears of relief...of grief...splash down your face.

She puts her arms around your neck and takes you fiercely into her world of devotion. She wants to make it better, to take away the hurt, and that's when you discover that above all else the hardest thing in the world is needing the courage of a breakable child to absolve your fears.

Night comes and you lay her down, in a bed of pink sheets and frilly pillows…of rich brown earth and bright moss, emerald green…and you kiss her forehead, warm and moist…cool and dry…You wipe away the saltwater that invades your eye, that comes from knowing it's over, that now she rests, at last, she sleeps…she sleeps…and that tomorrow, the morning will come…the mourning will come.

fiction entry

HOW TO PRAY

"This is how you should pray:
Our Father in heaven,
    let your name be kept holy.
    Let your kingdom come.
    Let your will be done on earth
        as it is done in heaven.
    Give us our daily bread today.
    Forgive us as we forgive others.
    Don't allow us to be tempted.
    Instead, rescue us from the evil one.
If you forgive the failures of others, your heavenly Father will also forgive you. But if you don't forgive others, your Father will not forgive your failures."
Matthew 6:9-14 God's Word Translation

The Call to Forgive

By Tyrean Martinson

I don't remember a time in my life when I didn't
believe in God. Even as a small child, I believed. I knew
God was real. I trusted in His light, His goodness, His
salvation. But I have often struggled with the call to
forgive.

It all started when a girl I met at church became my
best friend. We started spending a lot of time at each
other's houses. My friend's two older siblings started to do
terrible things to their two younger siblings and to any
other young children who came to their house (including
me). Eventually, even though they threatened to kill my
parents if I told anyone, I told a teacher at my school. My
friend found out I had told on her family and stopped
speaking to me. Her family started going to another church.
She told other kids at school that I was a tattletale and a
liar.

I lost many friends. I had been bullied before, but
without a solid tribe of friends, I didn't have any help to

fight them off. I began spending my lunch recess in the school library and found comfort in books, especially those that told me evil could be defeated with a bucket of water, a lion's roar, or an arrow to the heart of a dragon.

In Sunday School, we learned the Lord's Prayer and I struggled with it. "Forgive us our sins as we forgive those who sin against us." I didn't want to forgive. I felt ashamed and angry, daydreaming of unspeakable punishments for my friend's oldest siblings. The Lord's Prayer kept convicting me, so I started praying and asking God to help me want to forgive, even if I couldn't imagine forgiving them. I had night terrors nearly every night, struggled with trusting anyone, and just felt more comfortable with books than with people.

Books and a love of music gave me joy. I joined choir as a fifth grader. My parents took me to organ lessons, and although I didn't like playing organ, one of my teachers loved books. I admired her, because she encouraged me and had a heart full of faith. But, after she gave birth to her first child, she committed suicide. For the first time in my life, I doubted God's goodness.

I felt lost for a while. If I couldn't trust God, I wasn't sure who I could trust. After a year of depression, I got down on my knees and placed my trust in Jesus. I felt surrounded by God's love, forgiven.

Still, I still struggled to forgive others. I was bullied every day – name-calling, groping, tobacco chew spit on my locker, things thrown at me in the hallways. I persisted in school activities, school plays, track, clubs, and choir. I tried to pray my way through the hard stuff, but I was often angry.

I put dents in my locker with my fists when I lost my temper, until one day the school janitor very kindly asked me not to – he'd seen the bullying going on and had tried to stop it, but my school had some issues that ran deep into the administration and the social fabric of the community. I didn't tell my parents because I wanted to protect them, and because my mom was struggling with suicidal depression. I prayed every day for hours after school, pressing into faith. Friends began to help me. One of the guys who had previously bullied me became one of my defenders.

God entered in and helped me forgive a few people, then a few more. A guy who groped me in junior high asked for forgiveness at a Young Life meeting, and I gave it, easily, which surprised me as much as him. It felt like God worked a miracle on my heart. I felt freer. I started forgiving others, I accepted forgiveness a little more, and it got a little easier.

After high school, my childhood friend came to me and thanked me for reporting on her family. She told me there had been an investigation. Her oldest brother had been held accountable for molesting and raping six children under the age of nine. When she gave me her news, I felt relieved to know my report had mattered. I didn't completely forgive her oldest siblings then, but I kept working on it. I think I have forgiven them now, although when I wake from night terrors, the shame, fear, and anger are all back. I have to forgive again.

The shame of what happened to me feels like it's deep in my bones. When it hurts the most, it gets mixed up with the rest of my life and I sink into depression. It's not something I like to admit to anyone, but I know from experience, that when it gets bad, I have to seek help from a counselor. I wish I could just be fully healed, over and done with, but instead I'm on a slow path to wellness. God works in his own ways in each person's life.

God is mighty and powerful to save, my refuge in every trouble. He has forgiven me, and because of His forgiveness, I can forgive. I have forgiven. I will continue to forgive. It hasn't been a one-time and done thing for me.

It's a continuing action in Christ. Someday, maybe I'll graduate from forgiveness to another task, but for now, God seems to keep telling me to forgive and love in His name. And, in this, He is healing me. Every moment I turn to Him, He heals me, forgives me, renews me.

THE REASON I CAN STILL FIND HOPE

"The reason I can still find hope is that I keep this one
thing in mind:
>   the Lord's mercy.
>   We were not completely wiped out.
>   His compassion is never limited.
>   It is new every morning.
>   His faithfulness is great.
>   My soul can say, 'The Lord is my lot in life.
>   That is why I find hope in him.'
>   The Lord is good to those who wait for him,
>   to anyone who seeks help from him."
Lamentations 3:21-25 God's Word Translation

Broken, But Not Alone

By Melissa Posod

There are times in our lives where we will feel broken, alone and sad. Where it's hard to get out of bed and even answer text messages or emails. These times can feel long, dark and never ending. And sometimes these times are so dark that you don't see any light at the end of the tunnel. I have felt that way for months on end and I am forced to participate when I'd much rather sleep and be alone. Forced, because as a parent, you are needed and expected to do things. But when given the opportunity, I would sleep. I would sleep for as long as I could and as often as I could. I felt so fatigued and drained. I also didn't like anyone but felt alone. I was irritated and had little tolerance for almost everyone. From my husband to a stranger in line with me at the store. I was simply just a miserably depressed individual. I was filled with anxiety and a deep sadness. So much so, I planned to end my life.

In the winter months of 2017/2018, I sat in a darkness in which I had never felt before. I did not see any light at the end of this particular tunnel and even that scared me. My rational side knew I was in trouble. I found myself crying for no apparent reason, and sometimes for silly reasons. I literally wanted to sleep as much as possible to escape my reality but I also had to be a mom to my three boys, especially my youngest who was 4 1/2 at the time. I found myself stuck in a black hole where I'd try to go to church and smile and fake it but mostly just went hoping being there would help. But honestly, I lacked the faith in Jesus at the time and didn't expect him to help me. Now, just a quick back story on that. The reason I struggled with my faith was that I have always dealt with depression and anxiety for most of my adolescent years and I would beg him to take it from me. I'd sit in my closet asking him why and praying he'd make me happy. So, to me, the faith department was lacking a little substance. So, thoughts of being better off dead passed through my mind like ships through the ports, which was quite often.

I enveloped myself with sad songs and even sadder television shows or documentaries. My marriage was struggling and I felt distant from my kids. I felt very isolated from my family, who live in California and I don't see on a day to day basis anymore. Things were growing weaker internally for me and I started to plan how I would take my life. I thought about putting a gun to my head, but that would be so messy, and I would not want my kids to find me like that. And the chances of surviving that with brain damage was more likely. I thought about hanging myself, but there wasn't a place to do that in my garage or my house. And again, I wouldn't want my kids to find me. I then thought about the Narrows Bridge. How high up it was and the fact that my kids wouldn't have to find me. And that sounded like a better deal. I started to plan how I would jump. I would share my location with family on my iPhone so that they would hopefully be able to locate my body. Then I'd put my phone in a water tight bag, tape it to my chest with duct tape, leave a note taped to the side of the bridge railing, and voila! I would be free from the pain and anguish I was feeling. I would be forgiven by Jesus (in my mind) and welcomed into the gates of heaven.

But, before I could follow through with it, I found myself one night watching Netflix and came upon a documentary called, The Bridge. It was focused on the many people who took their lives on the Golden Gate bridge in San Francisco, California. It showed actual footage of people leaping to their deaths. But it also interviewed a couple people that had actually survived the jump - one being a man named Kevin Hines. And something about this man caught my attention. Something about his soul shone through, and the fact he lived to tell his amazing story. He said, "The second I let go of that railing, I regretted it."

When I heard Kevin say that, something clicked inside me. I immediately felt my heart change. I felt the heaviness leave my body and I knew I couldn't go through with it. I didn't miraculously feel happy but I felt something. I felt faith that I had lacked and trust in God that I was withholding. I went on to read his book and went to hear him speak at Peninsula High School about a year later. I got to meet him and thank him for sharing such a personal story with the world. It needs to be heard by many, and maybe only some with actually listen, but it saved my life. I see that in times of darkness, no matter how dark, no matter how hard, putting your faith in God takes the weight of it off you and allows light to creep upon you. Do not be afraid to allow others to know your story, to know your pain, and to see who you are beyond the smile. Because your story may help someone realize they are NOT alone.

LIGHT IN THE DARKNESS

"The people who walk in darkness will see a bright light.

The light will shine on those who live in the land of death's shadow."

Isaiah 9:2 God's Word Translation

The Light of Our Present God

By Ann Martin

I have always believed in God. His presence has lingered in the back of my mind. During my growing up years, I always had all of my needs and most of my wants met. Religion and the facts of a risen Savior were never discussed. My parents sent me to Sunday School, but it was not a fun place where a teacher told stories with flannel boards and taught us joyful songs.

The passing of my Dad opened a door, allowing me to go to college. Since where I was accepted was many miles from home, I had the freedom to choose my choice of church. It was at that point that I pretty much blanked out any religious thoughts.

I married and had children at a fairly young age. My new friends and neighbors attended a nearby church, but I still was not interested nor even felt a need.

When tragedy of a severe nature struck me and my young family, I was very aware of people all over praying for us. I was humbled by this. I also knew I needed to be finding strength and love from God on my own terms. I can remember crying and begging God to help me. I also remember the struggle I had hoping God could hear me. Did He even know me after my years of neglect? I asked for His guidance and calmness because people seemed to be coming at me from all angles.

God swiftly made His presence known. I was calmed and able to Let Go and Let God. He has shown me that He was always a part of my life.

I don't regret the years of a void in my life. I'm grateful that those dark times were eventually filled with the Light of our ever-present God.

THE BRIGHTNESS AFTER A RAINSTORM

"The God of Israel spoke to them.

The rock of Israel told me,

'The one who rules humans with justice rules with the fear of God.

He is like the morning light as the sun rises,

like the brightness after a rainstorm.

The rain makes the grass grow from the earth.'"

2 Samuel 23:3-4 God's Word Translation

Light Reflections

By Tyrean Martinson

Light reflections
On the underside of
   s c a t t e r e d
clouds,
   shimmering
the blue sky
    gold.

*previously published in Light Reflections: A
Collection of Poetry*

FAITH IS

"Now faith is the assurance of things hoped for, the conviction of things not seen. For by it the people of old received their commendation."

Hebrews 11:1-2 ESV

Real to Me

By Margaret Colman

When, Oh Lord, have you been real to me?
Shall I name the ways? Now let me see…

My reason for living was twice on the line,
The tumor I had that wasn't benign,
Gunmen that threatened to blow me away,
Yet faith didn't fail; you saved the day.

Life, new life, comes daily from you;
You died for me. I know it's true.
Sins I've taken to you in prayer.
Can forgiveness for these be possibly there?

I go to Communion, and what do I find?
Love in the eyes of one patient and kind.
I leave from there with hope in my heart.
Praise be to you! I'm given a new start!

A song is played, a hymn is sung,
Beautiful music, stirring everyone.
And somewhere in a melody,
A phrase comes straight from you to me.

Your Word is read, the Good News proclaimed;
Your message of love is always the same.
Yet when I hear the truth, and my heart says, Amen!
I am ever amazed that I believe, again.

Trials come my way, fears and worries, you know.
Sometimes it can be so hard to let go.
Then comes a peace. How can this be?
A brother or sister's been praying for me.

My family, Oh God, what a treasure they are!
My husband, our sons, dearest by far.

When I was lonely, feeling unloved,
You sent my husband, a gift from above.
In my best friend, you show that you care,
Acceptance, tenderness, all our days to share.

Our sons were born. Oh, the joy each gives!
Oh, what a piece of work he is!
So precious, so fragile, so very new,
Full of wonder and trust, in him I see you.

Your people show what you're like each day,
In little things that they do and say,
A listening ear, a gentle touch,
Laughter, smiles, that say so much.

My life is full of the ways you reveal,
How much you love me, how you are real.

Margaret Colman, March, 2000

99

AFTERWORD

Editing this book's details has been a privilege. It's a
joy to see the way our extraordinary Savior, Jesus Christ, is
at work in our ordinary lives.

It is my prayer that some of these words have brought
comfort, some have brought peace, some have challenged,
and some have brought hope. God gave His very own Son
to die for us, while we were still sinners. He loves us, and
nothing can separate us from His love. Thanks and Praise
to God Almighty! Thank you, Jesus, our Redeemer. Come,
Holy Spirit. Amen.

THANKS

I want to give a huge thanks to all of the members of One Hope Church, especially those who contributed here! Four of the authors here have been previously published. Otherwise, this is a work of regular people who answered a call to write their faith stories. I am so thankful for each and every one of you!

Plus, I want to thank Pastor Peter, Pastor D'Vante, and the team of Elders of One Hope Church who allowed me to collect these stories.

I give thanks to John Martinson, my husband, who helped me format the page numbers correctly, and who listens to all of my writer-editor ups and downs.

Finally, I want to thank Jesus Christ, again, for all the work He has accomplished and is accomplishing in our lives.

FINDING YOUR FAITH STORIES

Finding your faith stories just takes a few minutes of your time each day, during your prayer and reflection time at the beginning and ending of the day, or in spare moments you have to reflect in the midst of life events. Studying God's Word with prayer each day is a good way to connect with Jesus. Being a part of a Christian community also helps ground you in the reality of boots-on-the-ground kind of faith. We're all sinners saved only by God's grace. We remember that and celebrate that together in faith communities.

As you reflect on your prayers, studies, and life events (both big and small), just ask yourself this question: where do I see God working in this moment? Trust God to be there. He never leaves us or forsakes us, even when we can't see or feel him working in us, through us, and around us. Just press into Jesus, and ask him to reveal himself to you.

I recommend writing your faith stories down. Try keeping a God Journal. Write down where you see God at work in your life. Write down your prayers. Write down your praises. Write down Bible verses that touch your heart and why. If you don't see or feel God right away, just press into prayer and scripture. Know Jesus is with you. Keep seeking His light and goodness.

When you have some stories and you feel really brave, or just really ready, share your stories with someone you trust, or with a group of people who get who Jesus is. After that, try sharing with people who don't know Jesus.

Real stories from real people combined with the word of God are often a great way to share God's love with others. Our lives are a testimony of God's love and grace.

What do you do if you really struggle to write? There are other ways to see and share God's work in your life. If writing is an area of struggle, you can use talk to text or a recording method for audio or film. Take pictures. Paint. Collage. Sculpt. Garden. Dance. Speak. Create films. Sing. Make music. Build. Pray. God knows you and loves you, exactly as you are. He made you for such a time as this, right now, and gave you abundant gifts to share, so you can glorify His name.

Lord Creator, Savior, Redeemer, we thank and praise you for your glorious goodness and grace. We thank you for your abundant gifts. We ask for your help to see

your love and to share your love. Thank you, Jesus. Come,
Holy Spirit. Amen.